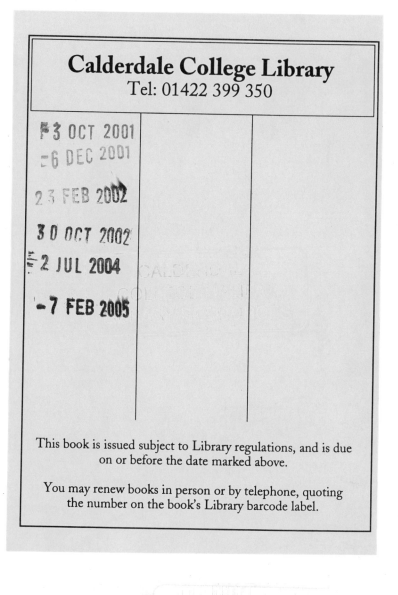

# Calderdale College Library
Tel: 01422 399 350

This book is issued subject to Library regulations, and is due on or before the date marked above.

You may renew books in person or by telephone, quoting the number on the book's Library barcode label.

# MAHATMA GANDHI

*The man who freed India and led
the world in non-violent change*

## Michael Nicholson

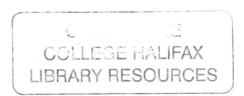
**🔢 EXLEY**

**Picture Credits:**
BBC Hulton Picture Library: 31, 42; Camera Press: 12, 26, 58, 59; Tom Hanley: 24, 25, 44, 52, 61; Indo-British Films Ltd: 20-1, 28-9, 32, 36-7, 40, 53, 57; the MacQuitty International Photographic Collection: 6 (top); National Army Museum: 15 (both), 30; National Gandhi Museum, New Delhi: 11, 13, 16, 19, 38 (below), 54, 56; Ann and Bury Peerless Slide Resources and Picture Library: 6 (below); the Photo Source: 4, 17, 43, 50, 55; Paul Popper Ltd: 38 (top), 48, 51; the Royal Commonwealth Society: 9 (both), 10; BK Sinha: 49.

The map on page 62 is reproduced by kind permission of the Press Information Bureau, Government of India. Our grateful thanks go to Sir Richard Attenborough and Indo-British Films Ltd for permission to reproduce stills from the film *Gandhi*.

Published in Great Britain in 1987
by Exley Publications Ltd
16 Chalk Hill, Watford, Herts WD1 4BN,
United Kingdom.
Second printing 1989
Third printing 1990

Copyright © Exley Publications Ltd, 1987

**British Library Cataloguing in Publication Data**
Nicholson, Michael.
  Mahatma Gandhi. –
  (People who have helped the world).
  1.  Gandhi, M.K. – Juvenile literature.
  2.  Statesman – India – Biography –
     Juvenile literature.
  I.  Title.
  II. Series.
  954.03'5'0924     DS481.G3

**ISBN 1-85015-091-5**

An abridged version of this title, with a reading level of 8-9 years, is available from LDA, Duke Street, Wisbech, Cambs PE13 2AE.

**Series conceived and edited by Helen Exley**
Picture research: Diana Briscoe.
Research: Margaret Montgomery.
Typeset by Brush Off Studios,
St Albans, Herts AL3 4PH.
Printed and bound in Hungary.

## FOREWORD

Mohandas Karamchand Gandhi is one of the most fascinating of history's great men. He did not start life with any special advantages. But at a very early age he made a rule for himself – that he would act in accordance with truth. And he took a vow – never to be pushed around. All of us make such resolves, but we break them easily. He stuck to them. He also decided that he would not use violence, even if others used it against him. Through insistence on truth and non-violence and also active opposition to injustice, he developed enormous power within himself. He attracted large numbers of followers. His example unlocked the power within them. It is said that he made heroes out of dust. This happened first in South Africa, where he went as a young lawyer and where he fought against racial discrimination. After he returned to India twenty years later, the entire people of his motherland ranged behind him as if he was a Pied Piper. They hailed him as Mahatma, or the Great Soul. He led them to freedom from colonial rule.

Mahatma Gandhi was a saint who was active in the world's affairs. He was a man of religion who preached equal respect for all faiths. He disavowed any new message and claimed that what he said was as old as the hills. He also insisted that what he did, others could do. He wanted people to accept his path only if they were convinced it was right. When his country became free he held no office or position. He owned no property. His wealth was the love he gave and got from the people. He was full of laughter and fun. In the midst of his battle against an empire, he had time to share the cares and pains of the humblest. He was totally unafraid of death. And when he was killed by a fanatic, he had the name of God on his lips.

This book should enable young readers to understand how Mahatma Gandhi helped the world.

*Rajiv Gandhi*
*Prime Minister of India*

# The watershed

None of us likes to feel unwanted. Even less do we like to have to take insults and abuse from others. In South Africa, Mohandas Gandhi was rapidly made aware that Indian people were disliked, unwanted and frequently insulted. Barbers refused to cut his hair. He was not allowed to stay in white hotels. He was attacked and beaten up by a stage coach driver when he refused to give up his seat to a white passenger.

Shortly after his arrival on a business visit to South Africa, Gandhi was put off a first class railway coach by a policeman acting at the request of a white passenger who refused to share a compartment with a brown-skinned Indian.

After being made to give up the seat for which he had a valid first class ticket, Gandhi had to spend the night shivering in a freezing station waiting room. That night he had plenty of time to consider his future as a new arrival in a hostile, unfriendly country. He had three options open to him. He could choose to ignore the insults and abuse and carry on regardless. Or he could go back to India as planned. Or he could decide to stay and fight racial prejudice. Gandhi decided it was his duty to stay and use his legal knowledge to fight for the black people of South Africa.

Gandhi described this early experience in South Africa as a watershed – a turning point in his life. He was a changed man, a man, moreover, who was born to change history. Now when we look back on his life, we can say it must surely have been a good thing that Gandhi was forced to endure the hardship and humiliations which so many of his fellow countrymen experienced all their lives. These experiences of injustice turned

*"It has always been a mystery to me how men can feel themselves honoured by the humiliation of their fellow beings."*
Mahatma Gandhi,
in South Africa.

*"I discovered that as a man and an Indian I had no rights. More correctly, I discovered that I had no right as a man because I was an Indian."*
Mahatma Gandhi,
in South Africa.

5

Gandhi's tomb with the Hindu inscription "Hey Rama." In English the nearest translation is "Oh God," the words Gandhi uttered as he died.

Right: Mahatma Gandhi's statue outside the house where he was born in Porbandar, India. There are statues and memorials throughout the land in memory of the man regarded by most Indians as their greatest leader and saint.

the shy young Indian lawyer (he was only 24 at the time) into a passionate fighter for human dignity and freedom. For the next 50 years he was to fight injustice, not with weapons, but with words and ideas, example and self-sacrifice. He developed *satyagraha*, a method of highly disciplined non-violent civil disobedience. In South Africa, and later in India, he taught his followers to face the British guns, bayonets and lathi sticks with highly organized, unarmed passive resistance. When the protesters, including thousands of women, were attacked and brutally beaten, they did not strike back. The people made fair demands of those in power and they were prepared to break unjust laws and go to jail – in their thousands.

His teachings were to spread from South Africa to India and eventually throughout the world. And after his death they still give people deprived of freedom and justice a way to fight oppression without having to kill. Martin Luther King, Greenpeace, the overthrow of Marcos in the Philippines ... today, we take protest demonstrations and disciplined pressure as the obvious way to fight wrong. Before Gandhi, the only successful way people knew to fight oppression was to organize a fighting force.

By the time of his death Gandhi had led the Indian nation to independence. Hitler had not been able to beat Great Britain's Churchill – but Gandhi had! This gentle, smiling man was revered by hundreds of millions of Indians but also by the leaders of the rest of the world. The United Nations, in an unprecedented move, halted its deliberations when the news of his death reached New York. They recognized that here was a rare man indeed, a man whose influence would last far beyond his lifetime. He had given a new tool to all oppressed people across the world. It was a weapon of love, not of death.

Einstein said of him: "Generations to come, it may be, will scarcely believe that such a one as this ever in flesh and blood walked upon this earth."

*"Mahatma Gandhi will go down in history on a par with Buddha and Jesus Christ."*
Viscount Louis Mountbatten
The last British Viceroy of India

*"To observe at first hand that mighty effort, to rub up against, if ever so briefly, the towering greatness, the goodness, the high spirits and humor, the humility, the subtlety of mind, the integrity and purity of purpose, and that indefinable thing, the genius, of this man was the greatest stroke of fortune that ever befell me."*
William L. Shirer,
Pulitzer Prize-winning author
of "The Rise and Fall of the Third Reich."

# Child of the Raj

Mohandas Karamchand Gandhi was born at Porbandar in India on October 2, 1869. India in those days was ruled by the British. There were at the time more than two hundred million people living in India, at least seven times as many as lived in Great Britain and Ireland.

Gandhi was born into a land of contrasts: of desert plains, vast rivers, swamps, arid plateaus, dense jungles and the highest mountains on earth. The climate of India is hot in the plains and cool in the highlands, but the vastness of India creates contrasts. India's peoples were separated from each other not only by the sheer difficulty of getting from one region to another but also by different habits, religions, and over 300 languages. Even peoples of the same race and religion were divided one group from another by their caste or station in life.

The British had been in India since the early seventeenth century when they set up trading posts by force, bribery, or in agreement with the Mogul Emperor and the local princes.

The British ruled over many races: people in the south with black skins, brown-skinned and pale-skinned people in the north. This was a land of princes and princelings, a land of great poverty and hunger and of vast riches. In India, those who were rich had to do nothing for themselves. There was always a servant to wash you, to shave you, to pour you a cool drink or fan you when you were hot.

There were many different religions in India. Most people were Hindus, though of many different sects. The Muslims, whose prophet was Mohammed and whose book was the *Koran*, were the second largest group. The Buddhists took their teachings from the Buddha who lived 2,500 years ago. A very old Christian Church, whose faith was first brought to India by St. Thomas, worshipped according to an ancient rite. Ancient communities of Jews had been in India for many centuries. There were also primitive tribal peoples

*Opposite: The India Gandhi grew up in was the India of the British Raj, with all its pomp, grandeur and ceremony. The British brought great organization and technical progress to India, but they were all too often insensitive to the people they ruled.*

*Top: The British King, George V, firing over the head of an elephant at a tiger in the grass, in 1911. His total kill was 24. His party killed 39 tigers, 18 rhinoceros and 4 bears.*

*Bottom: This is another photograph of the kind of India Gandhi experienced as a young man. It shows ceremonial mace-bearers in scarlet and gold livery at a Delhi durbar ceremony under British rule.*

European "gentlemen" had Indian servants who saw to all individual needs. The pay was four shillings a month (20p/30 cents) – less than half the wage for a similar position in England. This early photograph was taken in 1850 and shows a man being shaved by his personal servant.

of the hills and forests and the Parsees, who had originally come from Persia, who worshipped fire as a symbol of God.

Hindu peasants, who were mainly vegetarians, worshipped the cow. Muslims, some of whom would eat beef, regarded pig meat as unclean. A sect called the Jains, who covered their mouths in case they swallowed a fly, would not go out at night for fear of treading on a worm. The white hunter meanwhile, who could well have been a devout Christian, took delight in hunting the graceful tiger almost to vanishing point.

In 1869, the year of Gandhi's birth, the ties between Britain and India drew closer. The Suez Canal was opened and British ships no longer had to sail all the way around Africa to reach India. The grip of British power on India had tightened. The links of trade had been made even stronger. Because Britain had colonies over most of the world, it used to be said "the sun never sets on the British Empire" – it seemed then that the Empire might last forever. Yet by the time of Gandhi's death 78 years later, India had celebrated its independence from British rule. The gentle Gandhi was to play a great part in these important changes.

## Boy bridegroom

Mohandas Gandhi was his father Karamchand's fourth and last child. Mohandas was born into the *Vaisyu* caste which ranked number three out of four in Hindu society, though below the most respected *Brahmins* (or priests) and the *Kshatriyas*, the soldiers or rulers. Still his caste was much more privileged than the *Sudra* (worker) castes. Below them all were those who had no caste, the *untouchables* or "outcasts." These were the people who carried out the most unpleasant, dirty tasks in Hindu society – like cleaning the latrines. They were considered to be so low that caste Hindus thought they would be tainted if even their shadow was touched by an untouchable. These were the people Gandhi later called

*Gandhi at the age of 7. His main influence was his mother Putlibai, who was deeply religious. The principles she taught him marked his whole life.*

the Harijan or "Children of God."

Gandhi was a normal boy from a happy Hindu family, occasionally mischievous but no more than most. His father was a court official and became the first Minister of the small princely state of Porbandar. His mother, Putlibai, was a very religious Hindu who prayed at each meal and often fasted. She often visited the temple and did not care for luxuries and jewels. Gandhi would later become India's greatest spiritual leader and it was from this very early age that his mother's religious life had a deep influence on him.

There were books at home and life was comfortable enough. The whole family were strict vegetarians, but Gandhi was once persuaded by a Muslim boy to eat goats' meat. He told Gandhi that meat would make him grow tall and strong – strong enough to push the Englishmen out of India! In the mistaken belief that he would grow

*Mohandas Gandhi (right) and his older brother, photographed when Gandhi was 14.*

stronger, Gandhi tried eating goats' meat. It gave him horrific nightmares and he later deeply regretted the experiment.

Gandhi was a shy boy and he would often run home from school so that he did not have to speak to anyone. "I was always afraid lest anyone should poke fun at me," Gandhi remembered later. He loved taking long walks on his own and did not enjoy playing games.

When he was thirteen years old and still at school, Mohandas was married to Kasturba, the daughter of a Porbandar merchant. He had not been consulted about the marriage. As was the custom, and still is today in much of India, the parents of the young couple made all the arrangements and the bride and groom did not meet until the wedding. We may wonder how such a marriage could have a chance of success but for Mohandas and Kasturba it didn't seem strange and their marriage was to last for sixty-two years.

## Student in the heart of Empire

In 1888, at the age of nineteen, Gandhi set out on the three-week voyage to London where he was to study law. He was already a father: Harilal his first son had been born some months earlier. His student days were not particularly happy; he felt lonely, cut off from his family, and distant from his spiritual home. He had sworn that, while in London, he would touch neither wine nor women, and would keep to his strict vegetarianism. Gandhi's strict principles cut him off from many of his fellow students, making him feel even more isolated.

He wrote, "I would continually think of my home and country ... Everything was strange ... the people, their ways and even their dwellings. I was a complete novice in the matter of English etiquette and had continually to be on my guard." His vegetarian diet made things even more difficult. "Even the dishes I could eat were tasteless and insipid."

Still, like most young people Gandhi wanted to fit in as much as possible and to dress like his fellow students – in fact he went through a period of dressing in the fashion of the time. A fellow student recalled meeting Gandhi in Piccadilly Circus in London in 1890. Gandhi was "wearing a high silk top hat burnished bright, a stiff and starched white collar, a rather flashy tie displayed all the shades of the rainbow under which there was a fine striped silk shirt. He wore as his outer clothes a morning coat, a double-breasted waistcoat and dark striped trousers to match ... He also carried leather gloves and a silver-mounted stick."

This is an extraordinary contrast with the Gandhi the world came to know – the famous image of Gandhi dressed in his dhoti – a white home-spun cloth, simple sandles and a shawl.

*Gandhi as a young man, dressed in elegant European clothing. During his time at university in London he did not wear Indian national dress. It was more than ten years later when he again took to Indian-style dress. And then, he would dress as a holy man, in simple peasant garb.*

After two years and eight months in England, Gandhi passed his final examinations at the Inner Temple Inn of Court in London and was called to the bar in June, 1891. At just 22 years of age he had successfully completed his studies in French, Latin, Physics and Common and Roman Law. No doubt these studies helped train his mind but, though able and quick-witted, we cannot yet see in the young lawyer, who sailed back from England, the wisdom and resourcefulness which was to inspire millions. He did not look as though he was made of the stuff that would free the largest nation in the British Empire and inspire *millions* of people. He himself referred to his college days as "the time before I began to live."

## A new life in South Africa

On his return to India, Gandhi learned to his great sorrow that his mother had died. Gandhi had adored his mother and she had had a considerable spiritual influence on him. Influenced by her religious beliefs, Gandhi developed his own reverence for all forms of life and his teachings on pacifism and non-violence.

For nearly two years Gandhi tried to establish himself as a lawyer. The law practice was unsuccessful. He was given only one brief but when he stood up in Court in Bombay to argue the case, he became so nervous he was unable to speak. He sat down to the sound of laughter in the courtroom. Shortly after this Gandhi was offered the opportunity to represent a wealthy Indian merchant in South Africa, an opportunity which changed the whole of the rest of his life. He left to cover a single assignment but was to stay for twenty-one years.

Then, as now, South Africa was a deeply divided society. Black people outnumbered the whites by more than five to one. The whites were themselves divided and during Gandhi's time in South Africa, they were to fight a bitter civil war. As a community the hundred thousand or so Indian people in South Africa were despised. They

14

SPION'S KOP
NATAL
JAN. 24TH 1900

*Gandhi with the Indian Ambulance Corps in the Boer War, 1899. He served with distinction and led a thousand ambulance men. He and his followers believed this gesture of support for the British would mean the Indians would receive better treatment. They were wrong.*

had been imported to do lowly and disagreeable jobs which the black people would not do: mainly work on farms and growing sugar cane. These poor Indians, driven from home by semi-starvation, worked hard and lived in stinking wretched poverty. However, a few prospered and began to compete with the whites and for this they became hated and feared. Numerous government rules and laws were made attacking the Indians and removing their rights to vote, own land and move around freely.

Gandhi whose resolve was stiffened by his own experiences of racial injustice in his early days in South Africa, soon became a leader of the Indian community. By 1896, he was also a rich and successful lawyer earning more than £5,000 a year (worth over £100,000 in today's values!)

How then did Gandhi set about helping his people? Many of his ideas were practical and common sense. He set about making the Indians appear better people, more likeable, less strange to other people. He urged honesty in business so that they be trusted. He taught cleanliness and sanitation. He advised them to learn English so that they could talk to others. He urged them to drop their ideas about caste which separated one group from another.

On a trip back to India in 1896 to fetch his family, he wrote and published *The Green Pamphlet* which detailed Indian grievances in South Africa. Much indignation was aroused and, when he returned to South Africa in January 1897, he was attacked by a lynch mob. Under pressure from London, the Natal legislature later that year repealed the laws allowing racial discrimination in electoral rights and replaced it with an educational test.

Despite the fact that Gandhi was a pacifist, a man of peace, he taught that the Indians should accept the obligations of nationality. If the Indians wanted the rights of citizens of the Empire, they must accept the obligations of citizens of the Empire. In 1899 during the Boer War, although Gandhi sympathized with the Boers, he urged

Gandhi, with some of the staff he employed at his firm in Johannesburg, South Africa. Gandhi had a very profitable business and became very wealthy indeed. He was much admired by the South African Indian community because he was a highly educated barrister, with a law degree obtained in London.

the Indian community to support the British. He helped to form and train an Indian Ambulance Corps. He led a thousand ambulance men, who served with distinction.

In December 1902 Gandhi presented the Indian community's grievances to Joseph Chamberlain, the Colonial Secretary. Both Natal and the Transvaal were doing their best to drive the Indian community out. An Asiatic Department was set up in the Transvaal in 1903 and produced a stream of new rules and regulations over the next three years. Tension grew between Indians and whites but went into abeyance during the Zulu Campaign of 1906. Again, Gandhi offered his help to the government and organized another Indian Ambulance Corps. Marching up to 40 miles a day, they had to nurse a succession of flogged and wounded Zulus whom the white doctors and nurses would not touch!

## The first struggles

*"My public life began in 1893 in South Africa in troubled weather. My first contact with British authority in that country was not of a happy character. I discovered that as a man and an Indian I had no rights. More correctly, I discovered that I had no right as a man because I was an Indian.*
Mohandas K. Gandhi

In August 1907, the feelings of injustice in the Indian Community came to a head. The Black Act required that all Indian men and women had to register and be fingerprinted. Anyone without a certificate could be imprisoned, fined or deported. The Indians called these the "Black Laws" because they were unjust and aimed at black, brown and yellow people from Asia. Gandhi, though himself light brown in appearance, would often describe himself as black.

The Indian community was well aware of what the whites intended. At an election meeting in January 1907, General Botha had declared, "If my party is returned to office we will undertake to drive the coolies (Indians) out of the country within four years."

It was at this time that Gandhi first articulated the idea of *Satyagraha*, meaning "truth-force" or "love-force", which is "the vindication of truth not by the infliction of suffering on the opponent but on one's self." It requires self-control because the opponent must be "weaned from error by patience and sympathy." It is much more than "passive resistance" as it requires a constant positive interaction between the contestants with a view to their ultimate reconciliation. He made strict rules as to how the "Satyagrahis" should behave and trained his people during the South African passive resistance campaigns. There was to be no retaliation for insults, floggings or arrests. These were to be born patiently. The idea was to humiliate opponents, not to beat them, but to melt their hearts.

In January 1908, because he had deliberately refused to register under the new law and had urged thousands of others to defy registration Gandhi was sent to jail for two months. This was to be the first of many periods of imprisonment. He did not complain, but he was grateful to be given time for peaceful thoughts and reading. In fact he only served one month of the sentence.

To test the unjust laws on immigration, many Indians crossed the Transvaal borders illegally

Kasturba, three Gandhi sons and a nephew. This photograph was taken in about 1903 – the Gandhi's would finally have four sons. Kasturba couldn't read or write and she seemed to have little understanding of Gandhi's sophisticated and demanding course in life. Theirs was not a marriage of minds, yet they were very close and she stayed by his side and supported him in all he did.

Gandhi did so and was jailed twice more. Whenever the Indians felt they were being treated as second-class citizens, they quietly refused to co-operate and accepted their punishment.

In early 1913, Smuts went back on a promise to repeal oppressive taxes and the ban on Indian immigration; then a judge in the Cape Colony ruled that only Christian marriages were legal – all Indian wives thus became mistresses without any rights. For the first time, many women became involved in the civil disobedience campaign. The illegal border crossings into the Transvaal began again and a group of women called the "Natal Sisters" by Gandhi were arrested. Other Indian women from the Transvaal then made their way to Newcastle in Natal where they persuaded the Indian miners to lay down their tools and go on strike. Many thousands of Indians were arrested and sent to jail and, as the word spread, thousands more workers went on strike.

Gandhi led his people into the Transvaal and in four days he was arrested three times and finally imprisoned for three months. Gandhi as usual was happy to go to jail for as he put it, "the real road to ultimate happiness lies in going to jail and undergoing suffering there in the interests of one's own country and religion."

By the time that Gandhi called off the satyagraha campaign, he was known and respected throughout South Africa and India. The barrister who had once been unable to speak in court was a famous statesman known for his honesty, skill and courage.

And so, in June 1914, Gandhi and General Smuts, the great South African white leader and statesman, eventually came together and worked

Gandhi led striking miners, who were charged by British soldiers trying to disperse them. Gandhi told the men to lie down, believing that horses could not be forced to trample on people. He was right. During his time in South Africa, Gandhi pioneered new methods of non-violent civil disobedience and at one time almost a quarter of the Indian people of the Transvaal were in prison.

out a give-and-take agreement which gave the Indian community more dignity and self respect. Gandhi's campaign of civil disobedience had triumphed, the first such campaign which would ever triumph.

General Smuts pushed through the Indian Relief Act and at last after twenty years Gandhi felt free to return home. On parting, he sent General Smuts a pair of sandals he had made in prison. Smuts later said: "I have worn these sandals for many a summer since then, even though I may feel that I am not worthy to stand in the shoes of so great a man."

# A fundamental change

It was during the 21 years of struggle in South Africa that Gandhi developed even more profound spiritual beliefs. He had always been a Hindu, but now the great principles of the *Bhagavad Gita*, the beautiful and powerful Hindu book of scripture, permeated his way of life.

His beliefs would from now on affect his politics – and they would be dominant in *every* political decision he would ever take. They also affected the way he dressed, the way he ate – indeed, every facet of his life.

It is very difficult for non-Hindus to understand the principles Gandhi followed. Both in South Africa and later in India the British would misjudge his habits as "eccentric" and "faddish."

Gandhi was influenced by other religions and philosophies: he particularly liked Christian hymns. He loved Christ's teachings. Christ's Sermon on the Mount, he said, "went straight to the heart." "Blessed are the meek......" "Blessed be the poor for yours is the Kingdom of God....," "love your enemies...," "lay not up for yourselves treasures on earth..." These teachings of Christ were at the very heart of Gandhi's way of life.

He did not reject the other great religions and borrowed freely from the principles of other religious groups: Buddhists, Christians, Jains, Islams. In fact, partly because of this, he was an unorthodox Hindu and was hated by strict Hindus. It was, in fact, a strict orthodox Hindu who finally assassinated Gandhi because of his attempts to help the Muslims.

For Gandhi, one of the greatest principles, found in the *Bhagavad Gita*, was called *Samakhava*, which meant that people should not allow themselves to be upset by either pain or pleasure. They should work for right without fear of failure or hope of success. Gandhi always laid as much stress on the means as on the end. He paid great attention on *how* to bring about change.

Another great principle he followed was *Aparigraha*, which is non-possession of material things. Spiritual riches could be reached by being poor and uncluttered – without owning lots of goods. If you turn to the next page you will see a picture of Gandhi's sum possessions on his death.

*Ahimsa*, or non-violence to all living things is another great principle of Hinduism. This means non-injury to everything that lives. And so Gandhi would not eat animals or hurt them. He hated all violence and would not even kill, or allow to be killed, the deadly snakes sometimes found in the grounds around his home in South Africa. He would guide them away with sticks.

Gandhi's lasting legacy and most famous "weapon" was *Satyagraha*, "truth force." It was a word he coined which has come to be translated as non-violence or passive resistance.

Gandhi always sought truth and rejected anything hypocritical or false. He cultivated love and tolerance of other people and he was usually loved and deeply respected by the people he opposed.

He was always able to be at peace because of his ability to meditate. So that even when he was negotiating and working under great pressure – sleeping less than four hours a night – he was *always* cheerful, smiling and joking. His greatest opponents came to love him.

He changed a great deal in South Africa, trying to discipline his body and mind and to keep his greed, selfishness and lust for any kind of bodily pleasure in check. He had for example, become extremely successful and wealthy because of his legal skills. But he gave up all his wealth, including his home and fine clothes. He started an *ashram*, a communal farm similar to an Israeli kibbutz. He even tried to give away his wife Kasturba's jewels – which had been showered as gifts on the Gandhis by satisfied wealthy clients. This was especially unpopular with her because by tradition the jewels would be needed as wedding gifts for her daughters-in-law.

There were many other sacrifices Gandhi demanded from his family and his growing band of followers.

*"I have not the shadow of a doubt that any man or woman can achieve what I have, if he or she would make the same effort and cultivate the same hope and faith."*

Mohandas K. Gandhi

*Gandhi's ashram at Sevagram, where spinning is part of daily prayers. All food is grown on the site and the people lead a simple life of poverty. The Sevagram Ashram established by Gandhi is still in operation.*

Gandhi and Kasturba came to a mutual decision to take the vow of *Brahmacharya*. This means the complete cessation of all sexual activity. Gandhi felt that he had to rid himself of all physical desires in order to be at peace within himself and to be free under all circumstances, to help others and to act with love at all times.

So it was that during this period in South Africa Gandhi's whole lifestyle had changed. And the non-violent methods he pioneered and the political triumphs he had already achieved were based on these deep spiritual beliefs.

His religion would be even more important in the coming struggle for freedom in India. The rise of Indian nationalism would go hand in hand with a resurgence of Hinduism. Gandhi became the main instrument in *both* developments. Three quarters of the Indian people were Hindu and their religion had survived intact through wars foreign conquest and occupation. The Muslim had ruled India for centuries, but left Hinduism basically untouched. The large number of Christian missionaries had also made little impact. It was to be Gandhi's religious leadership *coupled with* his political craft which would enable him to bring freedom to India.

## Gandhi comes home

In January 1915 when Gandhi was forty-five, he returned home. He and Kasturba with their four young sons were surprised to be met by huge crowds when they docked. Gandhi's achievements in South Africa were famous and hundreds came to give him a warm welcome. The important people of Bombay held a grand reception to welcome him home.

Gandhi decided not to campaign for Indian rights until he had learned more about the problems in India. But he did set to work to establish

*A picture from Sevagram Ashram, showing Mahatma Gandhi's bed and belongings at the time of his death in 1948 – their value, £2.50p or $4. Gandhi's poverty and his way of life made personal criticism impossible for opponents. So it became a great political strength. It also made the millions of Indian peasants feel he was one of them and that he could lead and understand them.*

25

*Gandhi and Kasturba soon after their return to India in 1915. Gandhi now went barefoot and he would never again don Western shoes or clothing.*

his *ashram* at Sabarmati near the city of Ahmedabad. The men and women of the community, eventually about 200 of them, promised to live by Gandhi's rules. These were based on the religious principles he had taught himself to live by when he was in South Africa. Their lives were to be marked by honesty, truthfulness, celibacy and poverty. They were to eat a modest vegetarian diet. They were to lead a life of prayer and service to others.

You can imagine that ashram life could have become infuriating. All those rules! Saving paper and string and elastic bands. No luxuries. Yet Gandhiji* was such a warm, loving, charming person and his beliefs so compelling that people wanted to live with him and live his way. From this time he would never be short of followers.

Gandhi rapidly became known as a champion of the people's rights. He stuck up for the untouchables, the poor peasants and the poor factory workers in particular. He campaigned widely in early 1917 for the abolition of indentured workers going to South Africa. Later the same year, he was supporting the Indigo sharecroppers in Bihar against their British landlords, the farmers of Gujarat against taxes, and the mill-workers of Ahmedabad in a strike against their employers. So influential did he become that later in 1917, in the darkest days of World War I, he was summoned to Delhi. The Viceroy, the ruler of India, representative of the British, wanted Gandhi's assistance. To the great surprise of many pacifists Gandhi agreed to call for Indian volunteers to fight for Britain and the Empire.

Gandhi still believed that Britain was a force for good. He also believed, as he had in South Africa, that if the Indian people wanted the rights of the citizens of Empire they should serve the Empire if asked to do so.

So it was that volunteer Indian soldiers went to fight alongside British soldiers and those from the Dominions. The Indian soldiers fought in Mesopotamia and in Europe on the Western Front and many died in this cruel and wasteful war.

The Great War, as it became known, was to alter the course of history. The British and their allies finally won, but at a tremendous cost. Britain was severely weakened. Although few thought so at the time, the days of the British Empire were numbered.

The Indian soldiers knew they had earned the right to dignity, equality and self-respect. There was a new mood abroad.

Yet the Indian soldiers were to be disappointed. The understanding, the half promise of self-government Britain had given India during the War was not kept. Worse still the emergency war powers and restrictions on liberties were to be kept on after the war. Trial without jury and imprisonment without trial were to be retained; the Indian people felt cheated.

The old insensitivity of the British that Gandhi had seen in South Africa, was unchanged. It was obvious that the British had no intention at all of giving up their most popular and profitable colony.

*"I believe that I have rendered a service to India and England by showing in non-cooperation the way out of the unnatural state in which both are living. In my humble opinion, non-cooperation with evil is as much a duty as is cooperation with good."*

Gandhi, speaking at his trial.

## The first campaign

For the first time Gandhi decided to go against the British Government of India. He decided on a *hartal,* a kind of general strike. He proclaimed a day when no business was to be done. Stores were to stay shut. Employees were to strike. This began a 28-year struggle that would finally bring an end to British rule.

There was tremendous support for the hartals organized by Gandhi against the unjust laws. Unfortunately public protest turned into rioting in Delhi, Ahmedabad, Lahore and Amritsar. Gandhi denounced the trouble-makers and called off the whole campaign. Gandhi saw that the people had to be trained in obedience before civil disobedience could work.

As a penance for the violence and rioting, Gandhi announced he would fast for 72 hours and he called upon others to fast for 24 hours.

## The Amritsar massacre

April 13, 1919 was India's blackest day. A forbidden meeting was held at Amritsar, the sacred city of the Sikhs, in a large open space surrounded on 3 sides by high walls and known as the Jallianwalla Bagh. The local British Army Commander General Dyer, decided to suppress the assembly with the utmost brutality. Without any warning to disperse, he ordered a small force of native troops to fire into the unarmed crowd. There was no way to escape. *The soldiers fired for ten minutes leaving 379 people killed and more than*

*At the Sikh's holy city of Amritsar, the crowds gathered for a demonstration in sympathy with Gandhi's non-violent hartal. It was a religious festival and the crowd of men, women and children were in holiday mood. Without warning, the troops opened fire and hundreds were killed. This was the turning point for Gandhi – from then on he would oppose the British head-on. (From the film, "Gandhi.")*

1,200 wounded.

At least some of the lives may have been saved if General Dyer had not refused to allow Indian medics in to tend to the wounded.

Dyer said later: "I thought I would be doing a jolly lot of good." To the Commission of Enquiry, General Dyer said: "Yes, I think it quite possible that I could have dispersed them without firing, but I was going to punish them."

At Amritsar General Dyer also enforced the "Crawling Order." He ordered that in retaliation for the injury of an English missionary woman, soldiers should be posted with fixed bayonets

*In June 1920 Gandhi returned the war medals he'd received in South Africa. He wrote to the British Viceroy, "I can retain neither respect nor affection for a government which has been moving from wrong to wrong in order to defend its immorality."*

along the street where she lived. They ensured that *all Indians* had to crawl along the whole street on their bellies. It didn't matter if little old men had to pass down the street to reach their homes; hundreds had to crawl in the dirt and dust.

Most Indians – Gandhi included – felt totally humiliated by this. And it was something they would never forget.

Many British people, though not all, were deeply ashamed of General Dyer's deeds and of his various attempts at Amritsar to punish and humiliate the Indian people. The shock waves from the bloody event spread through the whole of India. The effect of Dyer's cruelty was to strengthen opposition to British rule. It also brought Gandhi into politics in a way he had never before sought or wanted: "I had faith in them – until 1919, but the Amritsar Massacre and other atrocities in the Punjab changed my heart." For the first time he began to see that British rule had to be overthrown. He returned his two British war medals and took on the leadership of the Indian nationalist movement. He realized that mere "self-rule" and "justice" were not enough. The British had to leave India.

## Congress reform

Before Gandhi joined it, the Indian National Congress was a kind of group of middle class windbags. Gandhi breathed new life into it and rapidly became its acknowledged leader. He turned it into a mass democratic organization with branches all over the country, even in the villages.

In December 1920, the Congress at Nagpur passed Gandhi's resolution calling for *Swaraj*, or self-rule, if possible inside the British Empire (like Canada or Australia), but outside the Empire if necessary. The Muslim leaders wanted to remain within the Empire and, after the resolution was passed, began to lose interest in the Congress. The Hindu and Muslim leaders started to drift apart.

At Nagpur in 1920 the Congress called for the

liberation of the "untouchables" and for the revival of village industries. Gandhi hated the way the untouchable caste were treated by the caste Hindus. He saw it as an insult and a threat to the Hindu religion. He wanted unity, unity based on equality.

## Spinning for victory

The collapsible spinning wheel was to become an article of faith to Gandhi and his followers. Its gentle and relaxing hum could be heard at Congress meetings or wherever nationalists gathered together. The spinning wheel was to become the symbol of liberation. It was practical. It was affordable. It made use of hands that had nothing else to do.

Gandhi saw in the spinning wheel and home weaving a way to revive the village economy and alleviate poverty. He attributed the desperate poverty of the Indian villages to the town dwellers and the British textile mills, which had destroyed the village craft industry. For the rest of his life Gandhi would spin 200 yards of yarn every single

*As part of a boycott of British goods, Gandhi urged Indians to spin their own cloth. Every day Gandhi would spin 200 yards of yarn. No matter how busy he was, he would never go to sleep until he had spun his daily quota.*

*Gandhi gave up the civil disobedience campaign after a group of his followers killed 22 policemen at Chauri Chaura. The demonstrators set fire to the police station, forcing the policemen out; they were hacked to death. This picture was a careful reconstruction of the event in the "Gandhi" film.*

day. Even if he was at an international conference or worked till 2 in the morning he would not sleep until he'd spun his daily quota. Basic education and a campaign for Hindi as a "national" language were also encouraged to help the national revival.

Gandhi, as he said himself, "turned the spotlight all over." In these months of whirlwind activity he turned to all kinds of problems. He was concerned with dirty streets, people spitting, rudeness on trains, neglect of poor farmers, and above all, violence.

During 1921, Gandhi went all over India – in third class railway compartments – spreading the message that non-cooperation would lead to independence. At vast public meetings he urged the people to give up wearing foreign clothing and to boycott British cloth.

His followers would strip off their foreign-made clothes and throw them into a fire and volunteers picketed stores selling British cloth. By this time Gandhi himself had permanently adopted his famous loincloth and carried a homespun bag. Unfortunately merchants' stock of foreign clothing were also set alight and fires of burning warehouses lit the sky at night. Gandhi did not approve.

In October 1921 a Congress working party called upon soldiers and civil servants to desert their posts. Lawyers were urged to give up their practices, and many did so. Schools and colleges were disrupted. More and more villages refused to pay taxes. By December 20,000 people had been imprisoned for civil disobedience and sedition.

The country was in a state of great excitement. Chaos was the order of the day. But amidst the fine expressions of pacifism and high ideals, there was growing disorder and violence on the streets. Even the British, who knew India well, were bemused and bewildered by the leading revolutionary activists. Especially by Gandhi. Gentle Mr Gandhi, middle-aged, dressed in a loincloth, always smiling his toothless smile, and by now attracting crowds of thousands of excited supporters wherever he went. They would walk for days just to see their great leader. As things came to the boil, rioting and disorder spread. Gandhi fasted as a penance for the violence. Then in February 1921, in the Chauri Chaura (United Provinces), 22 police constables were killed by an enraged mob during a campaign of mass disobedience. Gandhi was sickened by the atrocity and stopped the defiance of the government everywhere in India.

"It is better," said Gandhi, "to be charged with cowardice and weakness than to be guilty of denial of our oath and to sin against God. It is a million times better to *appear* untrue before the world than to be untrue to ourselves."

Many were disappointed, many felt let down, betrayed. But Gandhi was not prepared to sacrifice the principle of non-violence.

The first stage of the struggle was at an end. What had it achieved? In the first place Congress had flexed its muscles and demonstrated its power.

*"I came reluctantly to the conclusion that the British connection had made India more helpless than she was before, politically and economically. India has become so poor that she has little power of even resisting famines. Before the British advent, India spun and wove in her millions of cottages just the supplement she needed for adding to her meagre agricultural resources. This cottage industry, so vital to India's existence, has been mined by incredibly heartless and inhuman processes ... the profits and the brokerage are sucked from the masses."*

Mohandas K. Gandhi

There were obviously hundreds of thousands of people prepared to make great sacrifices, to give up their jobs and risk imprisonment in the cause of freedom.

But it only convinced Gandhi that for "non-violence" to succeed his supporters had to be highly trained and much more disciplined. He himself sought atonement for the murders in Chauri Chaura by going on a five-day fast.

For the British Government of India it meant that Congress could no longer be ignored. The demands of Indian nationalism had to be recognized and in some way satisfied.

The nationalists themselves felt a new strength. They had got rid of their inferiority complex and felt more able to deal with the Government on equal terms.

## Arrest and imprisonment

Shortly after the killings at Chauri Chaura, in March 1922, Gandhi was arrested. He was charged with rebellion against the government. At his trial, Gandhi, who described himself as a farmer and weaver, pleaded guilty. He made a long statement in which he said: "... *the section under which I am charged is one under which mere promotion of disaffection is a crime. I have studied some of the cases under it, and I know that some of the most loved of India's patriots have been convicted under it. I consider it a privilege, therefore, to be charged under that section ..... I hold it to be a virtue to be disaffected toward a government which in its totality has done more harm to India than any previous system. India is less manly under the British rule than she ever was before. Holding such a belief, I consider it a sin to have affection for the system.*

"*I am here therefore to invite and submit to the highest penalty that can be inflicted upon me for what in law is a deliberate crime and what appears to me to be the highest duty of a citizen.*"

Gandhi did receive the maximum sentence of six years and went cheerfully to prison again. He

"*We did not conquer India for the benefit of the Indians. We conquered India as the outlet of goods of Great Britain. We conquered India by the sword, and by the sword we should hold it.*"
Lord Brentford, 1930

told the trial judge he was grateful for the courtesy he had received during the trial. He had no regrets. "We must widen the prison gates," he said. "Freedom is to be wooed only inside prison walls." Happy in his prison cell Gandhi spent his time at peace with his books, spinning his wheel and saying his prayers. He was released in 1924 because of an operation for acute appendicitis.

When Gandhi came out of prison he discovered that the Indian National Congress was in disarray. The non-cooperation movement had collapsed. Even worse, there was much community unrest and bitterness between Muslims and Hindus. But Gandhi chose not to renew his campaign of civil disobedience until his prison sentence would have been served. Instead he devoted much of the next few years to trying to bring the two communities together.

In these quiet years Gandhi carried on preaching the virtues of the spinning wheel and the handloom. Gandhi said the wheel was like a restful prayer. He was accused of homespun fanaticism but he persisted. He said it was the great British textile mills and the Indian cities which had made the Indian countryside so poor. Gandhi urged his people to wear *khadi* or home-spun cloth. By buying *khadi* the townspeople would help the peasants. Home-spun was to be the link between town and country, rich and poor. The India of jewels and riches and silver and gold brocade was not Gandhi's India. Home-spun became the badge of the nationalists and the Congress Party.

## Civil disobedience

In 1929 Gandhi, now aged 60, turned again to the liberation of India. The new campaign of "civil disobedience" was to be different from the earlier campaign that had hoped to bring the government to a standstill by strikes and people pulling out of government jobs. That had failed, though it had given the Government a nasty jolt at the time.

The new campaign encouraged people to break the law. The mass arrests that would follow, would

*"Yes, but we have something more important than guns. We have truth and justice – and time – on our side.*
*"You cannot hold down much longer three hundred and fifty million people who are determined to be free. You will see!"*
Mohandas K. Gandhi

35

earn sympathy and gradually make government impossible.

Gandhi won the support of many doubters because of the sense of his position. He pointed out that over 80% of Indians were peasants – to win their support, it was essential to speak their languages, dress like them and understand their economic requirements and aspirations. They were far more likely to listen to an old man in a *khadi* loincloth and sandals speaking their own language, than to a Europeanized Congress member pontificating in English!

The new campaign started with a peaceful revolt against taxes. That ended with a total victory for the peasants. Throughout 1929, Gandhi toured India, speaking at rallies and organizing bonfires of foreign cloth.

But Gandhiji* had promised that he would declare himself "an Independence-wallah" if Dominion status was not achieved by December 31, 1929. Now he moved into action with his historic "Salt March."

## A pinch of salt

The climax to Gandhiji's much publicized Salt March, was when he quietly stooped and picked up a handful of salt. This simple gesture was the end result of Gandhi's carefully planned and disciplined 24-day, 200-mile march. Now over sixty and looking frail Gandhi had led his small band of 78 followers from his Sabarmati ashram to the sea. By the time they arrived several thousand villagers had joined them. The British treated it

*Gandhi had waited years before he unleashed another civil disobedience campaign – for he knew what power he held over the Indian people. He knew, too, how dangerous a non-violent campaign could be if discipline broke down. After carefully writing to the British Viceroy to give him a chance to back down, Gandhi launched the great campaign. He and a band of followers walked slowly, very slowly, to the sea – to pick up a handful of salt!*

* "ji" is added to the end of a name as a sign of affection and respect.

37

*Above: Gandhi on the Salt March.
He was with Mrs Sarojini Naidu, the
poet and his close associate. Gandhi
was soon arrested and Mrs Naidu led
2,500 protesters on the world-
famous and fateful Dharasana
Saltworks demonstration (see
overleaf.)*

*Right: Gandhi stooped for a handful
of salt. This symbolic gesture started
a nation-wide outbreak of civil
disobedience, as hundreds of
thousands of Indians broke the law by
producing their own salt.*

as a joke and dismissed the whole idea. Why was there any drama about picking up a handful of salt? Once again they underestimated Gandhi. They had no understanding of the feelings now running in India and they certainly had no understanding of how formidable and clever Mahatma Gandhi would be now that he was an outright opponent.

The idea behind the march was to inspire widespread civil disobedience to embarrass the government. The Salt Tax which Gandhi set out to destroy was not only a symbol of the Government's right to tax and therefore its right to rule – it was an emotional issue. The tax bore hardest on the poor, for no one, particularly in a hot country can live without salt. The poorest peasant was found to pay as much as the richest merchant. Many also thought that to tax a substance which nature provided free was especially repugnant.

Gandhi's flouting of the Salt Tax law gripped people's imaginations. Civil disobedience broke out in nearly every province. All over India poor people began taking salt from the sea. At least 60,000 people were arrested, including nearly all the Congress leaders.

On the night of May 5th Gandhi himself was arrested. He had been asleep under a mango tree near the seashore. The police came brandishing guns. Gandhi was quite calm, he brushed his teeth with a twig in the Indian way and allowed himself to be taken off. There was no trial and no sentence – he was simply locked away.

Gandhi had relied on being arrested; it was all part of the strategy.

## Satyagraha in action

Protests continued after Gandhi's imprisonment. Mrs Sarojini Naidu, the poet, led 2,500 Congress volunteers to the Dharasana Salt Works. This was defended by policemen armed with steel-shod staves. After prayers the protesters moved forward. The first column was headed by one of Gandhi's four sons, Manilal. They were viciously

*"... As we saw the abounding enthusiasm of the people and the way salt-making was spreading like a prairie fire, we felt a little abashed and ashamed for having questioned the efficacy of this method when it was first proposed by Gandhi. And we marvelled at the amazing knack of the man to impress the multitude and make it act in an organized way."*

Jawaharlal Nehru, leader of Congress and later India's first Prime Minister

attacked and beaten about the head by the soldiers. Obeying the rules of non-violence they did not defend themselves. They fell where they stood as the staves rained on their heads with sickening thuds. As the wounded fell with fractured skulls and concussion they were dragged away by women protesters. A second column drew up and in complete silence approached the stockade. The British officer barked an order and the police beat the protesters down. They were dragged away.

A new column formed.

*"They marched steadily, with heads up, without the encouragement of music or cheering or any possibility that they might escape serious injury or death. The police rushed out and methodically and mechanically beat down the column. There was no fight, no struggle; the marchers simply walked forward till struck down."** *

This was repeated, hour after hour. Two men died and 320 were injured.

This dreadful scene was witnessed by Webb Miller, an American journalist whose horrific account was published in more than a thousand newspapers. It did much to stir the conscience of Britain and the world about what was happening in India. Yet again, satyagraha was succeeding. The more unjust and cruel the British were, the more they played into Gandhi's hands.

Within a year Gandhi the "seditious fakir* was striding half naked up the steps of the Viceroy's Palace, there to negotiate and parley on equal terms with the representative of the King Emperor", to quote Churchill's angry comment.

The Viceroy, Lord Irwin, and Gandhi trusted each other. This series of talks resulted in what was known as the Irwin-Gandhi Pact. This was an agreement, among other things, to permit the free manufacture of salt. Civil disobedience was called off, prisoners were to be released and Congress was to be represented at the Second Imperial Conference in London in October 1930.

*Webb Miller's United Press eye witness account*

*A fakir is an Indian beggar monk*

*Opposite: The scene of the Dharasana Saltworks demonstration in the film, "Gandhi." It shows exactly how the 2,500 Gandhi followers, dressed in white, assembled in groups. Each group faced the 400 Indian policemen who carried 5 foot lathi sticks with steel tips. Wave after wave of demonstrators would assemble and wait peacefully to be beaten senseless.*

*"Europe has completely lost her former moral prestige in Asia. She is no longer regarded as the champion throughout the world of fair dealing and the exponent of high principle, but as the upholder of western race supremacy and the exploiter of those outside her own borders."*
Rabindranath Tagore, India's famous writer, who first called Gandhi the "Mahatma (Great Soul) in peasants' garb."

*"All hope of reconciling India with the British Empire is lost forever. I can understand any government taking people into custody and punishing them for breaches of the law, but I cannot understand how any government that calls itself civilized could deal as savagely and brutally, with nonviolent, unresisting men as the British have this morning."*
V.J. Patel, leader of the swaraj (self-rule) during Gandhi's arrest.

41

## The Round Table Conference

In August 1931, Gandhi sailed for Britain as the sole representative of the Indian National Congress. On embarkation Gandhiji warned: "I might come back empty handed." He didn't hope for much from the Conference. In truth he wasn't all that interested in the details of just how a new government should work. His was the human approach, and at the human level he scored a great success. He conquered the hearts of many British men and women and persuaded many more of the justice of his cause.

Newspaper headline writers loved him. When asked whether he had felt sufficiently clothed when he visited the King, he said, "The King had enough on for both of us." The English were intrigued by details of Gandhi's personal habits, his dress, his diet.

When he ventured into the cotton towns of Lancashire to explain his reasons for boycotting British cloth, Gandhi was cheered by the workers, many of whom were unemployed because of his policy. They liked the fact that Gandhi had taken the trouble to come and talk with them. This was something their own rulers rarely, if ever, did.

"Do you want your own prosperity to be built on the misery of others?" Gandhi asked them. And they said "No." He told them that they were much better off on their unemployment pay every week than an Indian worker who got less than half of that per *month* when he was working.

Gandhi was not a materialist. He did not value wealth but he hated grinding, desperate poverty. Gandhi said: "No sophistry, no jugglery in figures can explain away the evidence that the skeletons in many villages present to the naked eye. I have no doubt that both England and the town dwellers in India will have to answer, if there is a God above, for this crime against humanity which is perhaps unequalled in history ....

My ambition is no less than to convert the British people through non-violence and thus make them see the wrong they have done in India

*Gandhi arriving at 10 Downing Street, London, the home of the British Prime Minister. His informal Indian peasant's dress caused a great deal of publicity. But the British leaders were astounded at Gandhi's negotiating skills and unflagging energy. Always smiling and happy, he drafted resolutions, delivered talks in public and gave press interviews. He kept five secretaries busy and got only four hours' sleep a night.*

I do not seek to harm your people. I want to serve them even as I want to serve my own."

Gandhi's personal triumph was tremendous but the conference itself was a failure. In fact it was worse than a failure because it widened the differences between the Indians themselves. As Gandhi put it: "They went into the conference Muslim and Sikhs and Untouchables, and they came out of it Muslims and Sikhs and Untouchables – and never at any moment was the Indian nation there."

And so Gandhi – dejected but determined – left for India. He would never again return to Britain.

*Hundreds of thousands of Lancashire cotton workers had become unemployed because of the boycott and burning of British cloth, which Gandhi had led. Yet he was welcomed by the unemployed people and spoke to them about the far worse poverty in India. His listeners immediately realized that Gandhi not only sympathized with their problems but also had a precise grasp of detail of the cotton manufacturing industry.*

## "The Children of God"

Within three weeks of Mahatma Gandhi's return to India, he was back in jail. Once again, in prison he turned his attention to the untouchables, and

*A village of untouchables in Maharashta in western India. Gandhi thought that the caste system, and especially the treatment of the untouchables, was the worst aspect of Hinduism. He campaigned on their behalf and almost died on a fast to the death for improvements in their way of life. Gandhi called them the "Harijans" or "Children of God."*

began a fast to the death. His epic fast stirred the conscience of the people of India. Gandhi won some concessions from Congress about the way the untouchables were to be elected. More importantly, the effect of his fast was to improve the lot of the Harijan. They were not only touched but even embraced by their fellow Hindus. Wells and temples where they had not been allowed to go were now thrown open to them.

After his release from prison in 1933, Gandhi set out on a *twelve thousand mile* Harijan tour collecting money for the untouchables.

Gandhi was a very religious Hindu and believed that if you led a bad life you would come back to earth as a member of an inferior caste. But

Gandhi would not accept untouchability. As Gandhi said: "I know of no argument in favour of untouchability ... indeed I would reject all authority if it is in conflict with sober reason or the dictates of the heart."

Gandhi's fight for the untouchables was only partly successful. Yet the fight still goes on. To this day government officials and community leaders lead little bands of untouchables into tea shops and barber's shops; sometimes they are allowed back even when the officials have gone away again!

In these quiet years, Gandhiji took less direct action in Congress affairs and concentrated on welfare work. He also worked constantly on an issue which was central to him – Hindu/Muslim unity. The two groups were drifting further apart and Gandhi was heartbroken. He could see that independence would probably cause the final split. He would always say that independence should be delayed if there was any chance of avoiding that final rift.

*"To see the universal and all-pervading spirit of truth face to face one must be able to love the meanest of creatures as oneself."*
Gandhi, in his autobiography

*"I hold myself to be incapable of hating any being on earth. By a long course of prayerful discipline, I have ceased for over forty years to hate anybody. I know this is a big claim. Nevertheless, I make it in all humility."*
Mohandas K. Gandhi

## Storm clouds of war

If there was ever any doubt that the British would be forced to leave India within a few years, the events of 1939 settled the matter. India was not prepared for war. The rise of Fascism in Europe had seemed a faraway threat. Yet when war came it was to have a dramatic impact on Asian thinking.

On the whole India's Congress leaders supported Britain in her fight, but they resigned when the Viceroy decided that India was also at war without consulting them. To try to win Congress over, the British promised independence after the war, but Gandhi insisted on independence at once. In spite of this Gandhi was on the side of the Allies. He did not want to seize independence violently nor did he want to take advantage of Britain's difficulties. "We do not seek our independence out of Britain's ruin," he said.

In August 1942, Gandhi called upon the British

> *"You have been taught that the sum total of British rule in India is beneficial. Nothing is more false! You cannot escape two facts: first that under the British, India has become the world's poorest country; and second, that it is denied advantages and decencies to which any free country is entitled."*
>
> *Mohandas K. Gandhi*

to "Quit India." He told the All India Congress Committee "Our quarrel is not with the British people, we fight their imperialism." Perhaps Gandhi did not fully understand the significance of his action. Certainly he regretted the dreadful riots that followed his "Quit India" demand.

## Kasturba's death

Violence broke out again all over India when, two days after his "Quit India" speech, Gandhi was arrested and imprisoned yet again.

This was a time of great personal tragedy for Gandhi. Within a few days of his arrest, his devoted secretary Mahadev Desai died suddenly. Then his wife became sick. Gandhi and Kasturba, whom he called Ba, spent the last months of their lives together in prison. Their relationship, which had often been difficult when they were young, had now mellowed with age. Kasturba had come to be a significant influence on Gandhi's life even if only in the background. When death came, it was Gandhi who was holding her. Gandhi said: "I can say of the vacuum that has been created by Ba's death, it is something very different, a vacuum which cannot be filled." Ba had borne Gandhi four sons. And they had been together since they were children!

Six weeks after his wife's death, Gandhi was released from prison. He was very sick and the Viceroy feared more violence if he were to die in jail.

## The transfer of power

The Allied Victory in 1945 at the end of the Second World War marked the beginning of the end of colonialism. Britain was exhausted and the new Labour government was committed to Indian independence.

The British in India knew that time was running out. The Indian Civil Service had not recruited an English person since 1939. The Civil Service in India was getting old, tired and understaffed. It had had to deal with mounting food and cloth shortages, including a terrible famine in Bengal in 1943. Desperate poverty was widespread.

In 1945, the other Congress leaders were released from prison. In the elections that followed Congress kept its position as the largest political party but it no longer spoke for the Muslims. During the war, with Congress leaders in prison, Jinnah's Muslim League had gained increasing support for a Muslim state of Pakistan. The idea of "Partition", the division of India, was hated by Gandhi and Congress.

Britain's new Labour government decided to make a last attempt to preserve Indian unity and a cabinet mission was sent out to Delhi in 1946. Negotiations dragged on for three months but finally broke down because Congress and the Muslim League could not trust each other.

The Viceroy, Lord Wavell, invited Gandhi's disciple Jawaharlal Nehru to form an interim (temporary) government. Nehru asked Jinnah for his assistance in helping to run the government and offered the Muslim League several government posts. But Jinnah was unable to agree.

In August the Muslim League decided upon a "Direct Action Day" as a protest against "Congress Government" and to force the British to recognize their demand for a separate state. This led to a fearful outbreak of violence in the Calcutta region. Four thousand people were killed and 15,000 injured in a wave of shootings, stabbings and burnings. The bloodshed and murder spread to East Bengal. Muslim gangs went about killing and forcibly converting Hindus.

The news horrified Gandhi who decided to go himself and "to bury myself in East Bengal until such a time as the Hindus and Muslims learn to live together in peace. ... I do not know," he said, "what I shall be able to do there. All that I know is that I won't be at peace unless I go."

Gandhi himself described his mission as the most difficult in his whole life. When a colleague went to visit Gandhi in East Bengal, he found

*"The welcome was so disarming, his manner so friendly and radiant, that my nervousness evaporated before I could say a word." "... His gray eyes lit up and sharpened when they peered at you through his steel-rimmed spectacles and they softened when he lapsed, as he frequently did, into a mood of puckish humor. I was almost taken back by the gaiety in them. This was a man inwardly secure, who, despite the burdens he carried, the hardships he had endured, could chuckle at man's foibles, including his own."*
William L. Shirer,
in "Gandhi, a Memoir."

47

*An ugly riot in Bombay, showing a scene of communal Hindu-Muslim violence. Over half a million people were killed in the move to Independence. Had it not been for Gandhi, it is believed that the number of dead would have run into millions and a full-scale civil war would have developed.*

him in the house of a *dhobi*, a village washerman. "So there he was in the little hut of the village washerman, writing his letters by the light of a kerosene lamp." People found it heartbreaking to see the frail little man, now 77 years old, walking barefoot from village to village. But Gandhi threw every effort into his supreme task. He held prayer meetings, he received deputations; he preached courage, forgiveness and truth.

From Bengal Gandhi went to Bihar where the victims of the riots were Muslims rather than Hindus. By March Gandhi was holding prayer meetings, trying to get Muslims back in their homes and collecting money from Hindus for Muslim relief. He stayed in a small Muslim village, went on a half-fast and vowed he would not leave until Muslims and Hindus were at peace. One month later, the killings stopped.

## The last viceroy

The continuing disorder in India, despite the Mahatma's* efforts, made the British Government fearful. Jinnah still held out for partition and the resolve of Congress was weakening

*\* The Mahatma i.e. Gandhi. Mahatma means "great soul."*

Despairing of reaching agreement and horrified at the prospect of civil war, British Prime Minister Attlee took a bold decision: the British would hand over power no later than June 1948. The new and final Viceroy appointed for the job was Lord Louis Mountbatten. He had been World War II Supremo in the South East Asia Command and was a cousin of Britain's King George VI. Mountbatten came to the job youthful, fresh, informed and with complete authority. He arrived in Delhi in March 1947, and almost immediately sent word to Gandhi that he wished to see him.

Mountbatten said he would send a plane to pick him up but Gandhi insisted on going to Delhi in a third class railway compartment. Their first meeting was something of a surprise for Mountbatten. "Certainly I was quite unprepared

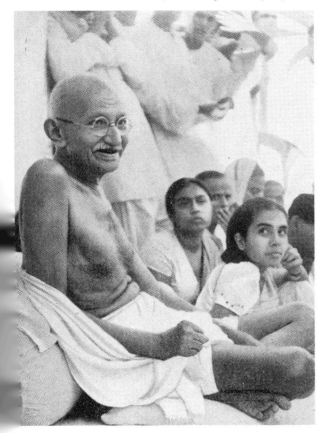

*Gandhi had gone to Noakhali in East Bengal to stop the massacres. When he heard of the mass killings – and arson, rape and religious atrocities – he said he would go there and die to stop the killing of Hindus by Muslims. He tramped from village to village, calming the people.*

*Lord Louis Mountbatten and Edwina Mountbatten invited Gandhi to tea on the lawn of the Viceroy's House. After three centuries of British rule, Lord Louis had come to India to preside over a rapid transition to independence – for a fifth of the world's population. Gandhi held no official position, yet he was the architect of the downfall of Empire, and Mountbatten recognised that only Gandhiji held the key to a peaceful change-over. He came to regard Gandhi as the greatest person he'd ever met: "His life was one of truth, toleration and love ... India, indeed the world, will not see the likes of him again, perhaps, for centuries."*

to meet such a lovable old man, with a warm, human manner; great good humour; charming manners, and perhaps most unexpectedly of all, an unfailing sense of humour. My wife and I welcomed him together, and friendly relations were effortlessly established."

Time was short. Mountbatten said "I could sense a real tragedy round the corner if we didn't act very fast – civil war in its worst form. Beside that, Partition, much as many of us hated it, seemed a much lesser evil. I could see no alternative." Partition was inevitable. And, inevitably, this also meant dividing two important regions with large Muslim populations; Bengal in the east and the Punjab in the west.

Working around the clock Mountbatten's team produced an Independence Plan in six weeks. Mohamed Ali Jinnah was not enthusiastic about it. Although he had insisted on Partition, he wasn't satisfied with what he called his "moth-eaten Pakistan." The main argument was over the two key provinces in Northern India, Bengal and the Punjab. Jinnah had insisted on Partition

*Gandhi and Lady Edwina enter the Viceroy's House for the negotiations. It was a heartbreaking time for Gandhi, as he tried to prevent the partition of India into separate Hindu and Muslim countries. After 30 years work, he was willing to postpone Independence to keep India united. But he lost, as mounting violence forced Mountbatten to accept the split.*

otherwise the Muslims would be swamped in Hindu India. Mountbatten and Congress said: "By the same argument, the two provinces you want in Pakistan, with large non-Muslim minorities, will also have to be partitioned."

Independence when it came, came fast. Many said too fast. Most of the princes were persuaded, bribed, cajoled or frightened into joining the new Indian States. Pakistan was to become a country of two parts separated by more than 800 miles. A lot has happened since then. The eastern part of Pakistan, East Bengal, broke away in 1971 and became Bangladesh.

*August 15 1947: Independence Day at the Red Fort in Delhi. Even though Gandhi had devoted 40 years of his life to lead the Indian people to independence, he would not attend the ceremony. He was in Calcutta fasting and working for peace between violent Hindu and Muslim groups.*

## Partition

For many of India's people August 15 1947 was one of the greatest days in history. One fifth of the population of the world gained independence that day. All the quarrels and animosities which had built up between the Indians and the British over the decades seemed to melt away. There was great rejoicing.

But Gandhi found nothing to celebrate. He felt "Partition of the Heart." "My independence," he said, "has not yet come ... there is no reason for festivals and merriments like this." Gandhi's idea of "unity" for which he had fought all his life had been rejected. He felt deserted by his fellow countrymen, abandoned by loved colleagues and friends.

Gandhi had always said he would like to live to be a hundred and twenty five years old. Now as the violence mounted and Hindus and Muslims started to kill each other he said at his praye meetings: "I wanted to be 125. Now I have lost interest in life." But even in these last months of his life, Gandhi still had more great battles to fight.

## "The old man has done it again"

August 1947 found Gandhi in Calcutta. Feeling sad and rejected himself Gandhi could still bring courage, comfort and forgiveness to others. Calcutta had already been through a year of terrible violence before Gandhi arrived. A well known Indian writer, Sudhin Datta remembered later, "For a year it had seemed as if it was not worth living in Calcutta. And then Gandhi had come. The first day I think they threw brickbats at him, and sticks at him, and then of course he talked to them, and slowly in two or three days time the atmosphere changed and on the 14th what we saw s perhaps the only miracle I have seen in my life."

*Twelve million people fled in opposite directions, as Muslims left India for the newly-created country of Pakistan, and Hindus fled Pakistan for India. (See map on page 62.) Over half a million people died in communal violence. This picture was a reconstruction of the exodus taken for the film "Gandhi".*

The "miracle" was Muslims and Hindus dancing and celebrating together and soldiers with little flags on their bayonets pinned on by the crowd. Everybody said: "The old man has done it again!"

Still Gandhi could not celebrate. By the end of the month violence again erupted and Gandhi himself just escaped injury. He told the people he would start a fast to the death in Calcutta to end only when the violence ended. Within four days the chief citizens of Calcutta brought him written promises of peace by their peoples and Gandhi was able to break his fast.

## One-man boundary force

That was in Bengal. In the Punjab in the North, where the authorities had also expected riots, 55,000 soldiers were stationed. They were overwhelmed by the violence and by the number of people who were forced to leave their homes.

*The British Viceroy, Lord Mountbatten, called Gandhi his "one man boundary force."*
*Thousands of troops could not stop the violence in East Bengal – but Gandhi did. He walked through mud and swamps to preach his method of non-violence. And everywhere he went he brought peace.*

Then Gandhi arrived. As Mountbatten said later, "When the trouble started the 55,000-man boundary force in the Punjab was swamped by riots, but my one-man boundary force brought peace in Bengal."

In September Gandhi undertook his last journey – back to Delhi. The capital city was ablaze with communal strife. There was murder and bloodshed. Refugees were fleeing from the old walled city as others were pouring in. This was just a small part of the mass movement of peoples taking place all over northern India. No one really knows how many lives were lost in these tragic weeks of violence, but a figure of 200,000 killed is probably too low! More than *fifteen million* fled from India to Pakistan or in the opposite direction.

Gandhi set to work. "I must do what I can to calm the heated atmosphere," he said. He visited the refugee camps; some housed Sikhs and Hindus driven out of the Punjab, some contained Muslims chased out of their homes in Delhi. His platform was the daily prayer meeting, which was usually held in the garden of Birla House where he was staying. His preaching and readings from the Hindu *Bhagavad Gita*, the Muslim *Koran* and the Jewish-Christian *Bible* were an inspiration. Hundreds attended, often thousands more listened on the radio.

## The last fast

Prayer was not enough. Gandhi felt he must do more. In January 1948, he announced his intention to begin a fast to the death. "The fast will end," he said, "when I am satisfied that there is a reunion of hearts of all communities." This, at the age of 78, his eighteenth great fast, was to be the final fast of his life.

By the third day of the fast the Indian Government was persuaded by Gandhi to make a considerable payment of money due to Pakistan. Many Hindus were outraged. They thought Gandhi was fasting to assist the Muslims who were at war with

*Three dead bodies lie unattended and unnoticed in the streets of Calcutta. Approximately three thousand people – mainly Muslims – had died during the previous five-day clash. Calcutta was the scene of the most violent clashes both before and during independence. It was only Gandhi who was able to calm Calcutta, and then only by another fast to the death. Yet again, he very nearly died. Yet again, he achieved his objective.*

*Gandhi with his two great-nieces, Manu and Abhu. He called them "my walking sticks" and they had cared for him since his wife, Kasturba's death. This photograph was taken the day before Gandhi's assassination. He was only just able to walk as he was recovering from his fast which had brought peace to the Delhi mobs.*

India in Kashmir. Crowds of refugee Sikhs and Hindus demonstrated outside Birla House, chanting "Blood for Blood" and "Let Gandhi die."

Gandhi was finally satisfied by the pledges given to him by the leaders of the different communities in Delhi. These representatives promised to restore communal peace and friendship by every possible effort, even at the cost of their own lives. Gandhi broke his fast on the sixth day.

Gandhi did not spare himself. Without allowing himself time to recover from the fast he went back to work. He was now working furiously on plans to give power to the people, and on many of his old ideas about putting life back into the villages. In the evenings he held the usual prayer meetings. At one of these, shortly after Gandhi broke his fast, a bomb was thrown. It injured nobody. But Patel, the Minister of Home Affairs, was fearful that Gandhi would be killed. He wanted everyone attending the prayer meetings to be searched; Gandhi refused.

"If I have to die, I should like to die at the prayer meeting. You are wrong in believing that you can protect me from harm. God is my Protector," Gandhi told Patel.

## The death of Gandhi

When Gandhi was a young lawyer fighting for Indian rights in South Africa, he was attacked by fellow Indians. One Muslim Indian who suspected him of betraying the cause threatened to kill him. Gandhi was not dismayed. Death held no fear for him. At that time Gandhi said, "Death is the appointed end of all life. To die by the hand of a brother rather than by disease ... cannot be for me a matter of sorrow and if I am free from thought of anger or hatred against my assailant I know that will rebound to my eternal welfare."

And so, forty years later it was to be.

Gandhi's thoughts about death were Hindu thoughts. He did not believe in a personal meeting with God, in fact he believed the self, the individual person would disappear. He thought o death as like the joining of streams and rivers to the sea.

On the last day of his life Gandhi rose in the cold clear Delhi dawn at 3 o'clock in the morning. Most of the day he worked, held meetings, and spent time in prayer. He was still at Birla House where he had entered on his final fast.

At about 5 o'clock that evening, after a meeting with Sardar Patel, Gandhi came out hurriedly from the house because he was a little late for evening prayers. Robert Stimson, a British correspondent who was there tells us: "He was wearing his usual white loin cloth and a pair of sandals. He had thrown a shawl round his chest for it was getting chilly. His arms were resting lightly on the shoulders of two companions and he was smiling. There were only two or three hundred people in the garden and they pressed eagerly towards him as he climbed the steps leading to the small raised lawn where the congregation had gathered. As he got to the top of the steps and approached the

*Each evening while he was in New Delhi, Gandhi would leave his quarters at Birla House to conduct evening prayers in the garden. On January 30, 1948, he was assassinated on his way to the waiting crowd. This photograph is from the film "Gandhi." The picture opposite is the actual scene of the Mahatma, with his great-nieces, on January 29, the day before his death.*

*A statue of Mahatma Gandhi in Delhi. In towns and villages throughout India there are statues in memory of the Mahatma. The inscription reads, "Believe in truth; think truth and live truth."*

crowd he took his arms from the shoulders of his friend and raised his hands in salutation. He was still smiling. A thick set man in his thirties I should say, and dressed in khaki was in the forefront of the crowd. He moved a step towards Mr Gandhi took out a revolver and fired several shots."

Gandhi murmured "Hey Rama" (Oh God) stood for a couple of seconds, blood oozing into his white clothes and at once he fell down and he was dead.

Lord Mountbatten told the author some year

ago what it was like to receive the news of Gandhi's death. "I was absolutely numbed and petrified," he said. "I went round at once to Birla House. There was a large crowd around the house already and inside it most of the members of government – everyone in tears. Gandhi looked very peaceful in death, but I dreaded what his death might bring.

"As I went into the house where his body was lying, someone in the crowd shouted out: 'It was a Muslim who did it!' I turned immediately and said: 'You fool, don't you know it was a Hindu?'

"Of course I didn't know – no one knew at that stage. But I did know this, if it was a Muslim, we were lost. There would be civil war without fail. Thank God it wasn't!"

It turned out to be a mad Hindu extremist – a young man from Poona, named Nathuram Godse, who was later hanged, along with another conspirator. Five others were sentenced to life imprisonment. Gandhi's funeral took place on the banks of the holy river Jumna at Rajghat where a million people waited for the cortege. Ramdas set fire to his father's funeral pyre, which burned for fourteen hours. Gandhi's ashes were then scattered in the sacred rivers of India and in the sea at Bombay.

Prime Minister Nehru, speaking on radio, had given the news of Gandhi's death to the Indian people shortly after the murder. "The light has gone out of our lives and there is darkness everywhere and I do not know what to tell you and how to say it. Our beloved leader, Bapu as we call him, the Father of our Nation, is now no more."

*Gandhi's personal belongings reflected his belief in non-possession. These were a few of the items he used at the time of his death: chappals (wooden sandals), cheap nickel-plated watch, spectacles, bowl, spoon and a book of songs.*

## Gandhi's gifts to India and the world

Nehru said, "The light has gone out, I said, and yet I was wrong. For the light that shone in this country was no ordinary light. The light that has illumined this country for this many years will illumine this country for many more years, and a thousand years later that light will be seen in this country, and the world will see it and it will give solace to innumerable hearts. For that light represented the living truth, and the eternal man was with us with his eternal truth reminding us of the right path, drawing us from error, taking this ancient country to freedom."

This surely is the point about Gandhiji. His was the light of reason, he was a beacon of sanity in an insane world. His was the voice of love, tolerance, and peace in this century of ultimate violence.

The little man in the loin cloth left behind far more than his modest possessions: his wire spectacles, his sandals, his nickle-plated watch, his stick, his twopenny chinese monkeys.

If it is true that the evil that men do lives after them, then so, surely does the good. The problem is we can't measure it.

Gandhi's great success in many ways was to prepare his people for independence. All his life he had taught truthfulness and cleanliness. He taught the Hindus proper pride in their own culture and traditions. He taught self-respect where before under the yoke of Empire there had been submissiveness. By the example of his own courage and fearlessness Gandhi taught his people to stand up for themselves.

Gandhi identified with the poor and they with him. He was loved by the factory workers, the poor peasants and the depressed classes for whom he consistently fought. He won the affection of many Muslims for his efforts on their behalf. He came to embody the true spirit of India.

Gandhi, in his loin cloth, visited the King of England at Buckingham Palace. The King asked him, "Mr Gandhi, how is India doing?" Gandhi replied pointing to his skinny limbs and his poor loin cloth, "Look at me, and you will know from me what India is like." Perhaps this was the secret of Gandhi's power and his mass appeal. Many Indians looked upon him as a real symbol of India. In his poverty and his humility he mirrored their lives. He could talk to them. He expressed their thoughts. He was one of them.

# Glossary

**Ahimsa:** The principle of non-violence in all thoughts and actions and therefore to all living creatures.
**Ashram:** A self-contained, usually religious, community.
**Boer War:** Fought in South Africa between the Boers and the British between 1899 and 1901.
**Brahmacharya:** A vow of perpetual celibacy (ie refraining from sex).
**Brahmin:** A member of the highest (or priestly) caste.
**Caste system:** a rigid system of hereditary social discrimination that divides into four main groups: *Brahmin*, *Kshatriya*, *Vaisya* and *Sudra*. Each group divides into thousands of smaller sub-groups that originally related to

occupation or rank. There are also the *Untouchables*.
**Civil disobedience:** A non-violent means of attempting to achieve political goals by refusing to pay taxes or obey laws. This is the usual form of *Satyagraha*.
**Congress, Indian National:** Founded to promote a role for native Indians in the government of India, it became increasingly politicized until it became the main organ of agitation for independence. It originally had Muslim participants as well, but is now a Hindu organization.
**Dharma:** A person's free will and therefore the obligation to do the best you can with your *Karma*.
**Darshan:** A Hindu concept describing how nearness to a holy man can influence followers for good.

**Dhoti:** Loin cloth.
**Harijan:** "Child of God" in Hindi; Gandhi's name for the *Untouchables*.
**Hartal:** A sort of national strike, where shops and businesses close as a political protest, but the day is spent in fasting and other religious practices.
**Hindu:** A follower of Hinduism, one of the four major religions of the world, which is the main religion of India. The religious conflict between Hindus and *Muslims* was the reason for *Partition*.
**Karma:** Fate or destiny. Another major tenet of Hinduism, it reinforces the *Caste system*, because it explains why a person is born into a specific caste.
**Khadi:** Home-spun cloth made on a hand wheel.
**Kshatriya:** A member of the

# The Indian sub-continent at independence, 1947

H. V. Hodson, *The Great Div[...]*
Hutchinson, 1969).

**PAKISTAN**

**INDIA**

Peshawar, Kashmir and Jammu, Srinagar, Rawalpindi, Lahore, Punjab, Simla, PS, Delhi, Baluchistan, R. Indus, Sutlej, Punjab States, Rajputana, Ajmer, NEPAL, BHUTAN, R. Brahmaputra, Assam, Shillong, Lucknow, Benares, Patna, Allahabad, Bihar, PAKISTAN, Dacca, ES, Karachi, Sind, Central India, Bengal, States of Western India, Central India, Ahmadabad, Central India, Calcutta, Porbander, Rajkot, GUJERAT, Baroda, Central Provinces, States, Nagpur, Wardha, Berar, Orissa, Cuttack, Bombay, MAHARASHTRA, Eastern States, Orissa, Hyderabad, Hyderabad, ANDRA PRAD ESH, Deccan States, Goa, Mysore, Madras, Madras, Cochin, Travancore

Boundaries between
India and Pakistan

International Province or State
of Provincial Status Boundaries

British India and
Leased Territories

Indian States

Tribal Areas

Italic names de[...]
regions designa[...]

PS = Punjab States   NWFP = North West Federal Province   ES = Eas[...] Sta[...]

*Before independence "India" referred to all the territories shown in this map. At independence the land was partitioned and the two mainly-Muslim territories separated from India and became Pakistan. Since then, East Pakistan has become Bangladesh.*

second (or warrior) caste.
**Mahatma:** "Great Soul" in Sanskrit; a title given to *Brahmin* sages and bestowed on Gandhi by the poet Rajath Tagore in 1916.
**Muslim:** A follower of Islam, one of the four great religions of the world.
**Pakistan:** The two areas in the north of the Indian sub-continent where *Muslims* predominated. East Pakistan gained independence after a war in 1971 and is now called Bangladesh.
**Partition:** The splitting of the Indian sub-continent

upon Independence in 1947 into India and *Pakistan* on approximately religious lines. More than 12,000,000 people fled across the new borders in one direction or the other.
**Purdah:** The custom of some *Muslim* and *Hindu* communities of keeping their women in seclusion.
**Satyagraha:** The force of "insisting on truth"; The name "Gandhi" coined for his policy of non-violent resistance to achieve a change in government or business policies.
**Sudra:** A member of the

lowest (or worker) caste.
**Untouchable:** A person of very low caste or who was completely outside the *Caste system.* They performed tasks such as road-sweeping and lavatory-cleaning that were regarded as polluting a high-caste Hindu beyond recall.
**Vaisya:** A member of the third (professional or merchant) caste.
**Viceroy:** The governor of a country or province who acts for and rules in the name of the sovereign.

# Important Dates

1869    Mohandas Karamchand Gandhi born on October 2 in Porbandar.

1882    Married to Kasturba. Both aged 13.

1888    Gandhi's first son, Harilal, born. Gandhi sails to England to study law.

1891    Returns to India after being called to the bar.

1892    His second son, Manilal, is born.

1893    In April, sails to South Africa to work for Dada Abdullah & Co.

1896    Returns to India to collect his family.

1897    His third son, Ramdas, is born.

1899-    Boer War: Gandhi supports British and organizes Ambulance Corps.
1901    His last son, Devadas, is born in 1900.

1904    Phoenix Farm purchased and Gandhi sets up his first ashram.

1906    Zulu Rebellion: Gandhi again organizes Ambulance Corps.

1908    First *Satyagraha* campaign begins in South Africa. Gandhi is sent to prison four times in next five years.

1913    South Africa repeals some of the discriminatory legislation against Indian community.

1915    Gandhi returns to India and founds an ashram at Ahmedabad.

1919    Gandhi calls a *hartal* for March 30 and April 6; the massacre at Amritsar occurs on April 10.

1922    Gandhi jailed in March for six years (released in February 1924).

1928    Congress calls for Independence for India.

1930    March: the Salt March to Dandi. Gandhi arrested in May just before Congress organizes the demonstration at the Dharsana Saltworks.

1931    Gandhi released in January and leaves for Round Table Conference in London.

1932    On his return to India, Gandhi is re-arrested (released in May 1933). September: starts fast to the death on untouchables issue.

1942    "Quit India" resolution passed by Congress. Gandhi and other leaders arrested.

1944    Kasturba dies in prison on February 22. Gandhi released in May.

1946    April: Jinnah calls for a separate Pakistan. August: Muslims massacre Hindus in Calcutta. Gandhi goes to the troubled areas.

1947    February: Lord Mountbatten appointed as last viceroy. August 15: Independence declared. September: Gandhi undertakes fast to the death against Hindu-Muslim violence.

1948    January 30: Gandhi assassinated by Nathuram Vinayak Godse.

# Index

## Further Reading

Gandhi, MK: *The Words of Gandhi, selected by Richard Attenborough.* New York: Newmarket Press, 1982.
Copley, A: *Gandhi, against the tide.* Kent, UK: Basil Blackwell, 1987.
Fischer, L: *The Life of Mahatma Gandhi.* London: Cape, 1951; Grafton, 1982.
Gold & Attenborough: *Gandhi; a pictorial biography.* New York: Newmarket Press, 1983.
Shirer, WL: *Gandhi, a memoir.* New York: Washington Square Press, 1982.